Citizenship

by Ann-Marie Kishel

first step nonfiction

Lerner Publications Company · Minneapolis

What does it mean to be
a **citizen**?

A citizen is a member of a country.

Someone born in the United States is a U.S. citizen.

Other people work to become U.S. citizens.

There are steps to becoming
a U.S. citizen.

First, people learn about the United States.

Then they take a test.

Finally, new citizens promise
to be good citizens.

Citizens have **responsibilities**.

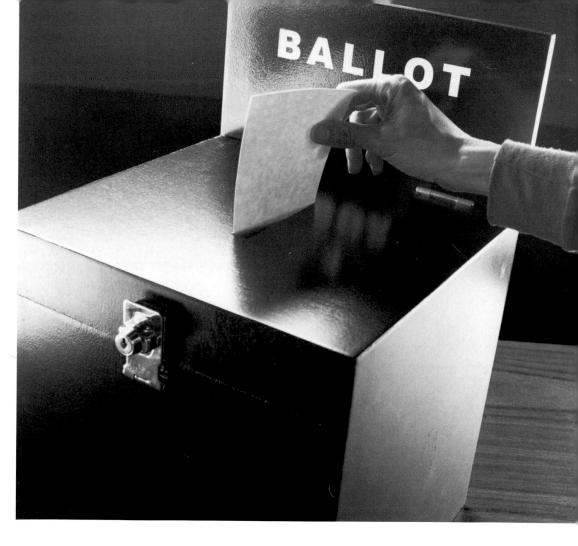

They **vote** for their leaders.

They obey **laws**.

Good citizens show respect
for others.

They work to make the
community a better place.

They care for the environment.

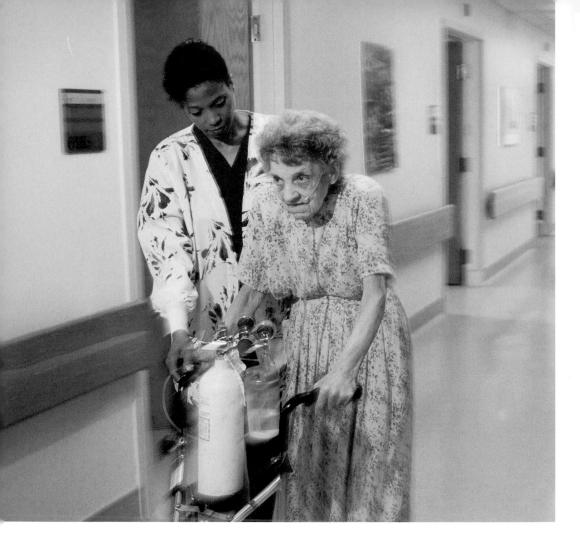

Citizens take care of one
another.

Are you a good citizen?

How to Become a U.S. Citizen

(If you were not born in the United States)

Learn about U.S. government.

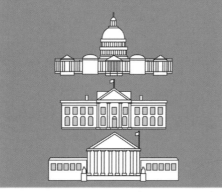

Learn about U.S. history.

Take a test.

Take the oath of citizenship.
Agree to be a good citizen.

Citizenship Facts

 An immigrant is a person who moves to a country from another country.

 The test to become a U.S. citizen has questions about the United States and its history.

 The Bill of Rights explains the rights of everyone living in the United States. It is not just the rights of citizens.

Learn about U.S. government.

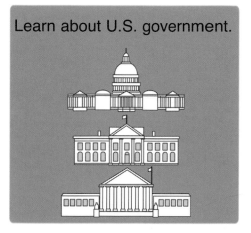

Learn about U.S. history.

Take a test.

Take the oath of citizenship.
Agree to be a good citizen.

Citizenship Facts

 An immigrant is a person who moves to a country from another country.

 The test to become a U.S. citizen has questions about the United States and its history.

 The Bill of Rights explains the rights of everyone living in the United States. It is not just the rights of citizens.

 The president of the United States has to be born in the United States.

 A citizen must be at least 18 years old in order to vote.

 Good citizens learn about elections. They understand what they are voting for.

Glossary

 citizen – an official member of a country

 community – the area where a group of people live

 laws – rules that tell us how we can act

 responsibilities – things that we should do

 vote – to make a choice

Index

The photographs in this book are reproduced with the permission of: Comstock Images, front cover; © Photodisc Green/Getty Images, pp. 2, 4; © Jeff Topping/Getty Images, pp. 3, 22 (top); © Karl Stolleis/Getty Images, p. 5; © Paula Bronstein/Getty Images, p. 6; © Digital Vision/Getty Images, pp. 7, 11, 17, 22 (bottom); © Jose Luis Pelaez, Inc./CORBIS, p. 8; © Paul J. Richards/AFP/Getty Images, p. 9; © Junko Kimura/Getty Images, pp. 10, 22 (second from bottom); © Blend Images/SuperStock, pp. 12, 22 (middle); © Randy Faris/CORBIS, p. 13; © Ted Spiegel/CORBIS, pp. 14, 22 (second from top); © Craig Hammell/CORBIS, p. 15; © Photodisc Blue/Getty Images, p. 16; Illustrations on pp. 18-19 by © Bill Hauser/Independent Picture Service.

Lerner Publishing Company
A division of Lerner Publishing Group
241 First Avenue North
Minneapolis, MN 55401 U.S.A.

Website address: www.lernerbooks.com

Library of Congress Cataloging-in-Publication Data

Kishel, Ann-Marie.
   Citizenship / by Ann-Marie Kishel.
        p.   cm. — (First step nonfiction)
      Includes index.
      ISBN-13: 978–0–8225–6398–3 (lib. bdg. : alk. paper)
      ISBN-10: 0–8225–6398–3 (lib. bdg. : alk. paper)
      1. Citizenship—United States—Juvenile literature. I. Title.
JK1759.K57 2007
323.60973—dc22   2006018514

Manufactured in the United States of America
1 2 3 4 5 6 – DP – 12 11 10 09 08 07